Ann Stow
3505 Tecumseh River Ro

ALEXANDER L. SHEFF

CENTURY EDITION

Speedwriting Publishing Co., Inc.

55 West 42nd Street, New York 36, N. Y.

NOTICE

You are now studying a course in "SPEEDWRITING" which identifies the best known and, in our opinion, the most efficient system of ABC shorthand. It is known throughout the United States and abroad under the distinguishing trade mark and service mark "SPEEDWRITING".

"SPEEDWRITING" is the registered trade mark of the School of Speedwriting, Inc. and identifies the books and publications of that organization and the term "SPEEDWRITING" means that system of instruction and teaching.

SPEEDWRITING
SHORTHAND

CENTURY EDITION

Copyright, 1923, 1925, 1950, 1951, 1954, by the Speedwriting Publishing Co., Inc. Copyrighted in the United States of America, Canada, and Great Britain.

ALL RIGHTS RESERVED

This book, or parts thereof, may not be reproduced in any form without permission of the publishers.

All rights to teach SPEEDWRITING shorthand from this book reserved to schools authorized by copyright owner.

Shorthand Plates Written by

Agnes J. de Vito

Printed in the United States of America.

CORRELATED LESSON EIGHT

16.

avenue	av	mortgaged	mtḡ
averaged	av̄	noon	n
Christmas	Xms	pair	pr
discounted	dis̄	post office	po
doctor	dr	railway	ry
evening	eve	secretary	sec
gallon	gal	square	sq
maximum	max	ultimo	ult
miscellaneous	msc		

ADDITIONAL WORDS

answered	ans̄	catalogs	cals
associated	aszā	credited	cr̄
assured	azū	crediting	cr̲
assuring	azu̲	credits	crs
avail	avl	dealing	dl̲
balanced	bal̄	figured	fḡ
barrels	brls	greatly	gl
bookkeeping	bkpg	likely	lkl
bought	bt	lined	lī

lining	li	pleasing	pz
monthly	-ol	retail	rtl
mud	-d	seal	sel
noted	nt	shape	zap
notice	nts	shipped	z
noticed	nts	shows	zz
numbered	no	slightly	-sl
placed	pl	surely	zul
placing	pl	wheel	-el
planned	pn	wishes	-zs
plate	pa	wool	-l

READING AND WRITING EXERCISE

A 1: .prsl -al b u co k th evl\ huv z l ro s av n pl v s sl\\ ub gl psl b. dla as uh pn lgi .hz f t ro\ n nl s.prsl a -k

la b. szs r rq\\ il ʒ.
—rdse bklou + iʒd lk lb
cr̄ f. asl v. sal\ ul

B ds: asu no r skl —n. lk
—re\ —nv ev. —rel lhlu v
.y. lk s lt̄ — —rd\ fe la
. —m —n —sp. skl p of.
—re ll n b. dla pv̄ v no
avl\ . flo hu —n —spl
.fnʒ lı + kl s hd\ hʒ kā f
b. dr asʒā —. skl\\ ev
—pn̄ a ʒo lrʒ —m, f —\
eʒ rʒ —m, f. skl as l\ l
u —p b a lkl? su

Now turn to Page 212 and complete the Writing Assignment.

BASIC LESSON NINE

18. Write *y* to express the sound *OI*.

boil	*byl*	joy	*jy*
boy	*by*	oil	*yl*
choice	*cys*	soil	*syl*
coils	*kyls*	toy	*ty*
join	*jyn*		

19. Write a comma to express the sound of initial and final *ST*. The comma for the initial *ST* is joined to the letter following the *ST*.

assist	*as,*	passed, past	*p,*
best	*b,*	post	*po,*
cast, cost	*k,*	rest	*r,*
earliest	*El,*	suggest	*sj,*
just	*j,*	test	*t,*
last, list	*l,*	trust	*T,*
lost	*l,*	waist, waste	*‿a,*
least	*le,*	stamp	*,‿p*
most	*‿o,*	state	*,a*
missed, must	*‿,*	stated	*,ā*

states	*sas*	still	*sl*
stating	*sa̲*	stock	*sk*
steal, steel	*sel*	study	*sd,*
step	*sp*	style	*sil*

20. Write *f* to express initial, medial, and final *FER*.

differ	*df*	refer	*rf*
offer	*of*	referred	*rf̄*
prefer	*pf*	referring	*rf̲*

DAYS OF THE WEEK

Sunday	*sn*	Thursday	*th*
Monday	*—m*	Friday	*f*
Tuesday	*tu*	Saturday	*st*
Wednesday	*—d*		

BRIEF FORMS

call	*kl*	several	*sv*
held	*hl*	table	*tab*
object	*ob*		

NOTE: *Indicate a proper noun by writing* ~ *under the word. Repeat a mark of punctuation at the end of a sentence to indicate a new paragraph.*

READING AND WRITING EXERCISE

A 1. i l, .by l — my lsl .bk f a lj s r v — m, \ ihop hl \

2. isp, la .b, rel f. — gd b a su — a fi — va, — vcek — sfr l a lok, \

3. — p sk . r, v . frl lyyn — re n hm o sn o — m \

4. .by as no cys \ h s l rd, f . l, o — d — o lh \

5. — n l u fnz . l, v . yl? l lh ra . el, ek fnz s b lu \

B 1 — el frnz . — sfn l k, \ lb ck bl f + sl m + ezz l l. el, u o — m \ e l, l l b no dla + la ll rec u — . mg o lu \ .dpl d lk las, u n gl l sl p o. — fo \ — p ra 1, — ezd bq \ su

Now turn to Page 214 and complete the Writing Assignment.

CORRELATED LESSON NINE

19. based ba,
coast ko,
discussed dsk,
earnest ~n,
fast f,
forced f,
finest fi,
greatest 7,
highest hi,
honest on,
insist ns,
largest · lj,
latest la,
leased le,
lowest lo,

nearest ne,
post po,
promised 7m,
protest 7l,
stage saj
stated sā
stating sa̲
stamped s⌣p̄
stay sa
stopped sp̄
staff } sf
stuff }
studying sd̲
waste ⌣a,

20. offered of̄
offering of̲
offers ofs

prefer 7f
refers rfs

ADDITIONAL WORDS

memo	—mo	tools	luls
occur	okr	type	lip
schedule	skdl	width	—dl
sheep	Zep	wife	—f

READING AND WRITING EXERCISE

A 1. Del rec . hu, lol v . y —n a ly
ln —l rz̄ . l, ps ic a lb\
2. agaq — —dl lul cos v Tū
l zp . ps rz hop la . k, d za
l . lol pvl l, y\
3. . za gvl as sk̄ la a abs
—zax o . ps v zel b st + .
— ps s b zd, —\

B j: br zf —ze l, —d e dsk,
. — ps psz̄ b . za\ e fl lal
—n b abz̄\ —o, v r dl s —

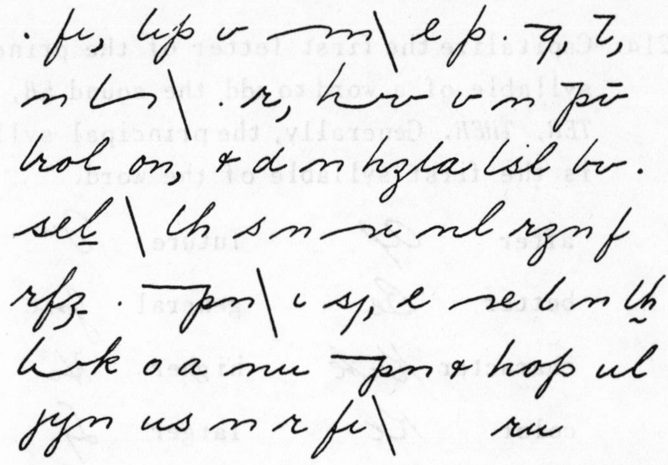

.fu, lfp o —m\ e p. q. l,
nl—\ .r, h—o o n pō
lrol on, + d —n hzla lsl b—.
sel \ lh s n—u nl rznf
rfz . —pn\ . sp, e —sel nlh
l—k o a —nu —pn + hop ul
fyn us n r fu\ —ru

Now turn to Page 216 and complete the Writing Assignment.

NOTICE

If the NATIONAL REGISTRATION FORM, Page 116, is missing from Book One when you receive it from the school, write immediately to:

Speedwriting Publishing Co., Inc.
55 West 42 St., New York 36, N. Y.

Unless this form is filled in by you and registered with the national office in New York City, YOU WILL LOSE ALL LIFE-TIME TRANSFER, BRUSH-UP AND EMPLOYMENT PRIVILEGES.

BASIC LESSON TEN

21*a*. Capitalize the first letter of the principal syllable of a word to add the sound *ER, DER, TER, THER*. Generally, the principal syllable is the first syllable of the word.

after	Af	future	Fu
better	Be	general	Jnl
character	Krk	higher	Hi
color	Kl	larger	Lj
cover	Kv	later	La
covered	Kv̄	longer	Lg
covering	Kv̲	lower	Lo
covers	Kvs	manner	Mn
discover	dsKv	material	Mal
*dollar	Dl	matter	Ma
either	E	member	Mb
ever	Ev	mother	Mo
every	Ev,	motor	Mo
favor	Fv	neither	Ne
further	Fr	never	Nv

*After a figure write d for dollars.

other	summer
paper	together
power	water
rather	weather
river	whether
similar	writer

21b. Combination *R* and *L* Series (Capitals). When an initial consonant or vowel is followed by *r*, join a hyphen to the capital letter

Ar	Er	Ir
Or	Ur	Tr
Br	Dr	Fr
Gr	Kr	Pr

When an initial consonant is followed by *l*, join a dash to the capital letter.

Bl	Fl	Gl
Kl	Pl	Sl

blower	clearer
brother	earlier

error	E	order	O
flower	Fw O	player	Pa
glamour	Gm	prior	Pi
grayer	Ga	sleeper	Sp
greater	G	tractor	Tk

BRIEF FORMS

deliver, -y	dl	opinion	opn
help	hp	over	V
labor	Lab	particular, -ly	Pl
latter	Ll	regular, -ly	rg
little	ll	turn	tn
newspaper	nzP	until	ul
open	op	voice	vy

READING AND WRITING EXERCISE

A 1. n. Tu i ppa bu Nal f a Ss Ko f. bd \ n Jnl ls Be f Ev, Ko lb Ssl n Kl \

2. n Ta No + Bo ppa G vy n. pls, v. nzP \ hv 1 Pl Nb d Ka n vys opn \

3. Lab d pfa Dl a r b kpll
l of nl a Hi ⌣kl ra\

4. . Ki lk a Lq li lgi s opn n
. Na\ hd ln los Ja f hp
n . Na\

5. ihop ul ⌣a ul . lVe s
‾Ke f a sal dn . Kv\

B ds: ek dl u rq nz lou du
. Sn l a lo k,\ no O co
k du lh l a Lo fq\ ifu du
n dla r ps s n.l 50c
⌣kl\ sk lb p o r l, f .
dl v . po,\ lh of s op lou
f nl a ⌣k\ f lh lls n
ur a rq ∩ ib\ dp a
ck n . ⌣al + . lp l rec
u b lh\ ul

CORRELATED LESSON TEN

21a.

boiler	Byl	feature	Fe
bother	Bo	federal	Fdl
butter	B	fiber	Fb
chamber	Cmb	folder	Fol
chapter	Cp	former	Fm
cheaper	Cp	formerly	Fml
collar	Kl	furthermore	Fmo
collateral	kLl	generally	Jnl
colored	Kl̄	greater	G
covered	Kv̄	honor	On
covering	Kv̲	jobber	Jb
dealer	Dl	junior	Jn
debtor	Dt	leather	Le
dinner	Dn	ledger	Lj
easier	Ez	liberal	Lbl
elevator	Elva	lumber	Lmb
familiar	Fml	materially	Mal
favored	Fv̄	natural	Nal
favors	Fvs	naturally	Nal

nature	rubber
officer	*shipper
officers	silver
ordered	smaller
ordering	sooner
orders	sugar
others	teacher
owner	timber
papers	upper
poultry	voucher
recovered	

21*b*.	flour	proper
	flower	traveller

* *When a Speedwriting outline starts with a capital letter, add r to express the sound ER.*

READING AND WRITING EXERCISE

A ds: ev rlz la r kb Cps

lobgf. rg re pl \ e pn

lbld a Lg kb h s \ a Cp

nb hz Bo s Drk v a l,

co as of thpgl a rg \ e n

gl a ro Lbl of l a Cp ra

f n. gvl \ h v edv Cpa

kz f. ll \ d u p k lo.

nbs Dr lo Fr k V lh

na \ uvl

B j: . Nav . bldg bs s sc la ekn

ll va l okrn. Fu \ ls Ke

ln Ev la pssl rzb Ls \ . Lg

u va . so ulv Cpa f nal

+ Lab \ as u pn lbld

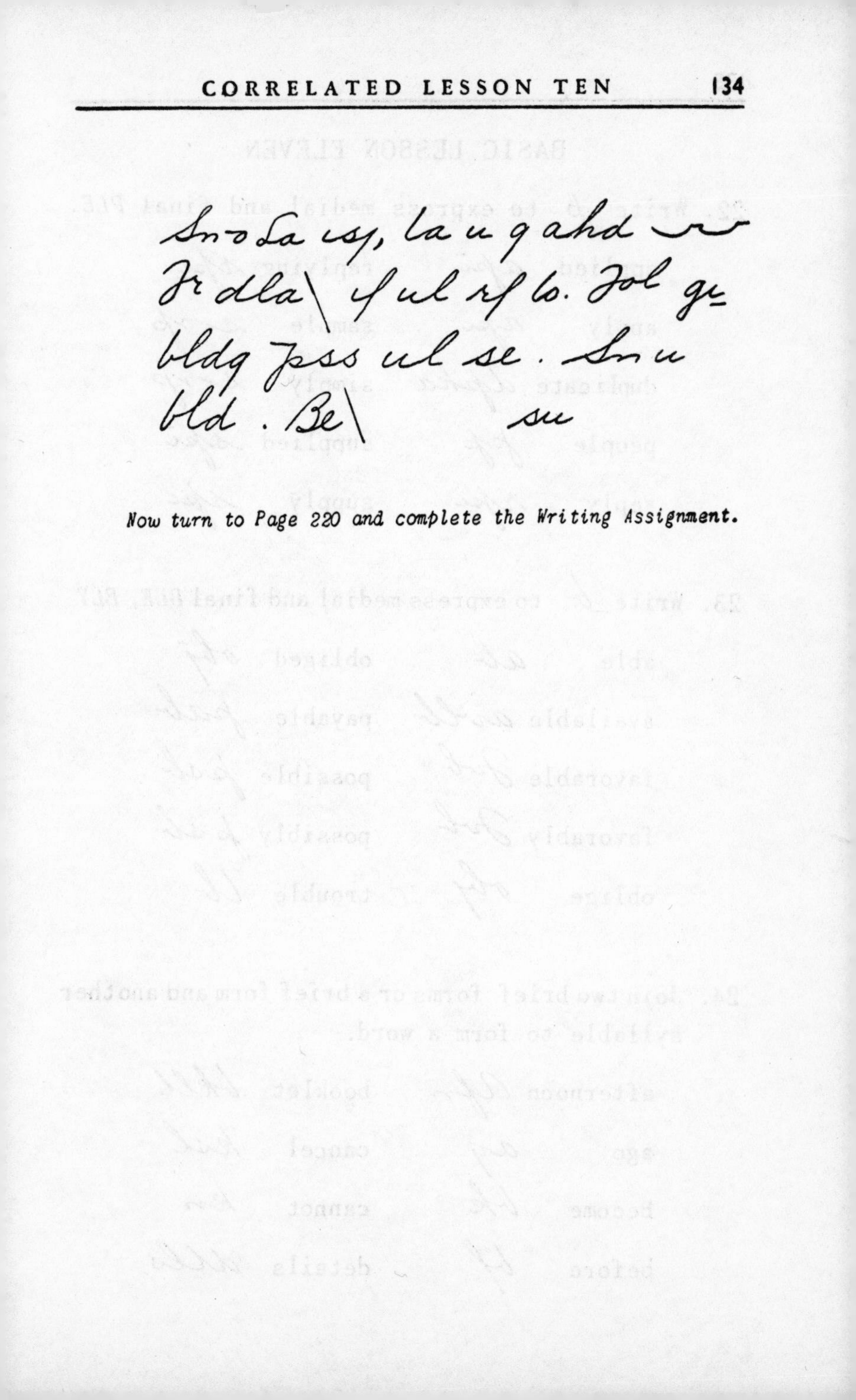

Now turn to Page 220 and complete the Writing Assignment.

BASIC LESSON ELEVEN

22. Write *p* to express medial and final *PLE*.

applied	*apī*	replying	*rpi̲*
apply	*api*	sample	*smp*
duplicate	*dpka*	simply	*smp*
people	*pp*	supplied	*spī*
reply	*rpi*	supply	*spi*

23. Write *b* to express medial and final *BLE, BLY*

able	*ab*	obliged	*obj̄*
available	*avlb*	payable	*pab*
favorable	*Fvb*	possible	*psb*
favorably	*Fvb*	possibly	*psb*
oblige	*obj*	trouble	*Tb*

24. Join two brief forms or a brief form and another syllable to form a word.

afternoon	*afn*	booklet	*bklt*
ago	*ag*	cancel	*ksl*
become	*bk*	cannot	*kn*
before	*bf*	details	*dtls*

everything	Ev̲	return	rtn
force	fs	returned	rtn̄
form	f	returning	rtn̲
herewith	he	sometime	s-tk
inasmuch	nsc	somewhat	s-a
inform	nf	therefore	Tf
into	nt	today	td
invoice	nvy	within	-n

READING AND WRITING EXERCISE

A 1. sl psb fu lspi -se - a dpka bl n O lpa . -se o -n . ku u l?

2. sv -os aq wy -n opn bf ispī u - . lab a s-p v -c aps o pq3\

3. as v td lu Tf ksl n O f dl v . -o\ ikn q nt . dlls n-\

4. lsa s-sp ?af. sgr bln
.sdse -c s-l avlb\ -p
nf-s --s v. lb n lh ?a\

5. ns-cs cfl n. f-s l,
-o + dd ngl. -sdse cfd
lk lksl -n ? as v ld\

B 1. ilnhe- -sdse spī lose
du. p, -k+ -?lnfs u la
ikn psb dpkal\

2. ks. ps v sel s fx uv no cys
n. ?a\ -na -o lh ps ln
b n fs\

3. . bal v. -lq du o. bldq s
pab -na y?s -\

4. o st sv Ɩ nbs — v. opn la ʒ ʒ —m, avlb lpa. slq\ lh ʒ a s—va ʒvb vu\

5. isp, u nfsu frs v. Ɩb uv h n spi rel\

Now turn to Page 222 and complete the Writing Assignment.

CORRELATED LESSON ELEVEN

22. applies apis | replied rpī
applying apī | replies rpis
couple kp | simply smp
duplicate dpka | supplies spis
pupils pups

23. assembly asmb | profitable pfīb
cable kb | reliable rlib
capable kpb | reasonable, -bly rznb
double db | suitable sub
label lb | tablet tbl
liable lib | valuable vlub
problems pbms

24.

Word	Shorthand	Word	Shorthand
accompany	aco	hereafter	heaf
became	bk	hereto	het
becomes	bks	heretofore	hef
becoming	bk	high school	hiskl
behalf	bhf	highway	hi-a
belief	blf	ideal	idl
belongs	blgs	informing	nf-
below	blo	income	nk
canceled	ksl̄	likewise	lkz
canceling	ksl-	membership	mbz
carload	kald	northwest	NW
chairman	ca-	otherwise	Oz
elsewhere	ls-r	outfit	oufl
everybody	Ev,bd,	outfits	oufls
everyone	Ev,1	outline	oule
foreign	fn	overcharge	vcq
forget	fgt	overdue	vdu
formal	fml	overlook	vlo
forth	ft	oversight	vsi

ownership	Onz	therein	In
recall	rkl	thereof	Iv
removal	rml	thereon	Io
removed	rmv	thereto	It
renew	rnu	tonight	tni
renewal	rnul	typewriter	tpri
replace	rpl	warehouse	rahs
salesman	sls-	welcome	lk
salesmen	slsm	whatsoever	asv
somebody	sbd,	whereabouts	rabs
someone	s1	whereas	rs
sometimes	stis	whereby	rb
thereafter	Iaf	wherein	rn
thereby	Ib	wholesale	hlsl

READING AND WRITING EXERCISE

A d —ra: . pups v NW
hskl r —pn a sub —a
lOn , v l ? Ics\ ?s rl
kpb v lec b ks v h af ?s obj

lgi p lec l Nl \ v. pups
d lk lgi a Dn n h On\ l u
p rpi & ll se f ur ab
las, . dlls & s v.
pb s\ su

B dbl: ulb placo rs
ga lo. Dn\ s v h D
pups v of l bq D s f
h lab\ af Dn. ca l
rkl. kpb lec ? as dn\ bn
l lb s bd, lsq f us\ nh
bhf ev rz m, lgl h a
Slo lvl kk\ l lb a
lbl c l sa s p "a lc
el Nv fgl\" su

Now turn to Page 224 and complete the Writing Assignment.

BASIC LESSON TWELVE

25. Write a / to express medial or final *RD, RT, WARD.*

according	ak/_	heard	h/
*accordingly	ak/_l	hard, hurt	h/
art	a/	part	p/
assorted	as/¯	party	p/,
board	b/	record	rk/
card	k/	regard	rg/
certain	s/n	report	rp/
certainly	s/nl	short	z/
court	k/	shortage	z/j
courtesy	k/s,	sort	s/
effort	ef/	support	sp/
forward	f/	toward	t/
forwarded	f/¯	word	‿/
forwarding	f/_	yard	y/

* *The ending INGLY is expressed by attaching the l to the underscore.*

26. Write a hyphen to express the sound of medial or final *NT, MENT*.

agent	aj-	present	pz-
current	kr-	president	pzd-
development	dvlp-	print	p-
different	df-	recent	rs-
don't	do-	recently	rs-l
event	ev-	sent	s-
evidently	evd-l	settlement	stl-
front	f-	shipment	sh-
judgment	jj-	statement	sa-
moment	-o-	sufficient	sfsh-
paint	pa-	want	w-
payment	pa-	wanted	w=
plant	-p-	winter	w=
point	py-		

27. Write q to express the medial or final sound *NK*.

bank	bq	thank, think	tq
blank	-bq	thanking	tq-
drinking	-dq-	thinking	tq-

BRIEF FORMS

advertise	avz	find	fi
America, American	a	happen	hp
		kind	ki
approximate, -ly	apx	magazine	mag
child	ci	necessary, -ly	nec
children	cil	result	rsl
collect	kk	succeed, success, -ful, -ly	suc
communicate	kuka		
country	K	upon	pn
describe, description	des	world	wo

READING AND WRITING EXERCISE

A 1. lgu fu ck n sll- v u kr-
bl\ el cr. pa-lou fr\

2. m s/n la. pzd- l py-
losfz- sp/ fr. K f s pn\

3. nars- z- u ap- s- a s/n
spi v pa- f r Ss hs\

4 as p/ v . rk/ ly h/ . rp/ o .
?/ spi v b/ f . dvlp-\
k/s, ?d avz a A lo. ?o\
? s/n u ? lsp/ lhy-\

ds: ?d lk ldes . rs- ?-
v pa- u s- lose f n U-
spi\ l aps lb a ?/ n bu
+ _r\ s/nl ur n ?/ v lz
Kls n u p-\ ? vu n lq
la a ad ?- v . nec Kls ?n?
n O lb s- lqu fu el n
lh ?a\ u

Now turn to Page 226 and complete the Writing Assignment

CORRELATED LESSON TWELVE

	Word	Shorthand	Word	Shorthand
25.	accord	ak/	forwarding	f/̲
	garden	g/n	guard	g/
	carton	k/n	hardly	h/l
	cord	k/	heart	h/
	fortunate	f/na	pardon	p/n
	forwarded	f/̄	regarding	rg/̲
26.	acknowledgement	ak-	center	S-
	advertisement	avz-	central	S-l
	anticipate	a-spa	development	dvlp-
	anticipated	a-spā	didn't	dd-
	anticipating	a-spa̲	disappoint	dspy-
	apartment	ap/-	disappointed	dspy=
	appointment	apy--	document	dk-
	argument	‾ag-	doesn't	dz-
	assignment	asn-	efficient	efz-
	assortment	as/-	evident	evd-
	can't	k-	garment	gr-
	cement	s-	grant	‾g-

guarantee	gr-e	presenting	pz=
haven't	v-	prevent	pv-
isn't	s-	printed	p=
joint	jy-	printing	p=
maintain	m-n	prominent	pm-
management	mj-	student	sd-
meant	m-	sufficiently	sfʒ-l
merchant	mrc-	supplement	sp-
painted	pa=	urgent	uj-
patent	pt-	wanted	=
pleasant	pz-	warrant	r-
patient	pʒ-	won't	o-
presented	pz=		

READING AND WRITING EXERCISE

A j: avz mn no ls nec lbas
jj- o rlib dla\ e ppā dla
o Ev, pt- ful + o Ev, p- bll
du. y\ e ga a yl sp- o Ev,

bq ra-lo\\ n ak-.pzd-v
a gr-frs rus"u s/nl du
a q jb v kk dla\ ls nec
f -e lgl.apx nlj v lv, fn
?- + lv, pa- -q= lu gvl ps
sp/ + ckp nfī lu u -rol
rp/"\\ u lo l -- . ro,
rs- rp/ o Ev, nu dolp-\
lgl a 7e kp, -sal . atc
k/\ olu

ds: ?e ns/. avz- ab u
bldg n r -kl o -rol -raq?
uk q/ ag dspy-- b sl .
avz- n lj lp\ . des v .
bldg s q b vf . sal s up-
e sp, a -ro pm- hd\
u -n lz ab gr . ps lo\
su

THERE IS NO WRITING ASSIGNMENT FOR THIS LESSON

BASIC LESSON THIRTEEN

28. Write a dash to express the sound of medial or final *ND*.

beyond	by—	handling	h—l̲
bond	b—	land	l—
demanded	d⌒—=	mind	⌒u—
depend	dp—	round	rw—
end	e—	send	s—
friend	f—	sending	s—=
found	fw—	sound	sw—
ground	gw—	stand	ɀ—
hand	h—	standard	ɀ—/
handle	h—l	window	⌣w—o
handled	h—l̄		

29. Add *s* to form the plural of words ending in a letter of the alphabet. Repeat a mark of punctuation at the end of words to form the plural.

amounts	a⌒ls	cases	kass
bills	bls	checks	cks
boys	bys	finds	fes

follows	flos	samples	s-ps
goods	gs	sizes	szs
invoices	nvys	stamps	s-ps
its	ls	stocks	sks
rates	ras	times	ls
agents	aj--	regards	rg//
statements	sa--	reports	rp//
wants	---	copies	kp,,
hands	h——	parties	p/,,
cards	k//	costs	k,,
parts	p//	tests	l,,
records	rk//		

30. Write s to express medial *ST*.

custom	ks-	mistake	-sk
customer	Ks-	postage	psj
customers	Ks-s	system	ss-
estimate	es-a	tested	ls̄
listed	ls̄	trusted	Ts̄
listing	ls̲	trusting	Ts̲

READING AND WRITING EXERCISE

A 1. k idp— pn u lv. ʒ-s-b
ʒa l ips ⌐—/ lu?

2. l u kcl des. psv l— u af--
avʒ n. nʒl ld?

3. — ps— se a des v. ks
+ b—— u h—l \ lv n
u— nl la ʒus\

4. .ks v lh fr s lh—l
⌐—/ dsel fa pss\

5. . p/,, lolh rp/ fr la . esra
gr s s— n lv, rq/ \

B 1. . sk n. psprs ad apx
10c lo. k, v. kp,, es- lor Ks \

2. n O ls— ou opn . rag
ʒ s- lolv, p/ v . K \

3. n, ssr v k// la u h— l d
dp— pn. kis v rk// e
dr— \

4. . dr— f rks + b— — dp— —
pn. ra v nk ly gi \

5. ev fr— th srp ssr lb
suc n bs n rs, p// v.
K \

Now turn to Page 228 and complete the Writing Assignment.

NOTICE

If the NATIONAL REGISTRATION FORM, Page 116, is missing from Book One when you receive it from the school, write immediately to:

Speedwriting Publishing Co., Inc.
55 West 42 St., New York 36, N. Y.

Unless this form is filled in by you and registered with the national office in New York City, YOU WILL LOSE ALL LIFE-TIME TRANSFER, BRUSH-UP AND EMPLOYMENT PRIVILEGES.

CORRELATED LESSON THIRTEEN

28. attend — fund
attended — handed
attending — intend
band — intended
binding — pending
bound — refund
brand — render
calendar — send
candy — sending
cylinder — standing
depending — standpoint
dividend — windows
ending — wonder
friendly — wondering

29. booklets — goes
businesses — its
cars — lines
creditors — lots

	months	⌣os	weights	⌣as
	notes	nls	works	⌣ks
	notices	nlss	bonds	b——
	offices	ofss	friends	f——
	plates	—pas	grounds	g⌣——
	sales	sals	duties	dl,,
	sells	sls	ladies	ld,,
	sets	sls	studies	ɹd,,
	states	ɹas	plants	—p--
	styles	ɹls	points	py--
	suits	sus	students	ɹd--
	taxes	lxs	shipments	ʃ--
	things	lgs	suggests	sj,,
	times	lis	towards	l//
	towns	l⌣ns	words	⌣//
	ways	⌣as	proceedings	—psd̳
30.	assistant	ass-	hasten	hsn
	estate	esa	installed	nsl̄
	estimated	es ɹā	installing	nsl̲

justly jsl outstanding ous=

listing ls postal psl

mistaken -skn trustee Tse

misunderstanding -sUs=

understanding Us=

READING AND WRITING EXERCISE

A ds: e Us— la u ⌣ Z
Uh— l r h & r s= r
cal ls ⌣ / rls & szs o
⌣— os\ ⌣— os sg o r—
—a b dzn̄ ls O\ n sc
kass pa- Zd b d—=
⌣n. O s pl̄ sola T s no
—sUs=\ ⌣n a fu -os
r nu avz- l ap n ous=
-ags\ b/ly ap o. nzs——
nlsslb s- ou lor ap--\

f . 2 — py- v avz- e gu r
Dls as —rc salshp asek\
o . bssv sals ek sa la ev
. lp, sl̲ —v— o n . —vo\
vlu

B ds: er hp, lnfr u v u apy--
as1se v sevu skl \ a
oul v u dl,, lbs- u lq
—nls o . psd v. l, re̲\
l . e— v ec Kl— y ulb
obj lal— a Jnl re̲ lfu
ou . es rā k, v —s— n̲
bldgs + gr—— + —asv
rz f——\ r psd-s——
u s ku, rq//\ su

Now turn to Page 230 and complete the Writing Assignment.

BASIC LESSON FOURTEEN

31. Write the right or closing parenthesis) to express final *ITY*.

ability	ab)	locality	lkl)
capacity	kps)	probability	pb)
city	s)		

32. Write the apostrophe (') to indicate final *SS, NESS*.

class	k'	happiness	hp'
discuss	dsk'	illness	l'
dress	d'	less, loss	l'
greatness	g'	mass, miss	m'
guess	g'	pass	p'

33. Write *k* to express initial and medial *COM, CON, COR, COUN, CUM*.

account	akt	common	kn
accounts	akts	complete	kpe
comfort	kf/	confident	kfd-
commit	kt	consider	Ks
committee	k)	considerable	Ksb

convenient	kvn-	recommend	rk—
county	kt,		

BRIEF FORMS

almost	lmo	liberty	Lb
already	lr	life	lf
also	lso	nice	ns
always	lw	organize }	og
avoid	avy	organization }	og
both	bo	represent }	rep
busy	bz	representative }	rep
charge	~~cq~~ cj	thought	tt
easy	ez	throughout	Tu
learn	ln		

READING AND WRITING EXERCISE

A 1. us — gd lln la u rep ltl
Lb lk + se us\

2. lw ks ~a s kvn- fu bf u
kpe. nec rp/ \

3. vzd lk ldsk' u l' bfug lo k' \ p k n ls kvn-fu \

4. n kfd-la u z lavy . cq la ur lobz ldsk' . k) rp \

5. fu k lo. b, v u ab) ul ful ez Un lh s s v ru \

B 1. ek n rec . s) f r lkl) n a ll l' ln a r \ ls v ez lgl lor h s \

2. n ur n lobz r rep l klo u lq V u akl \

3. lu . y e k lo. b, v r kps) \ h v er hp, lgl a kpe r, l. e— v . y \

4. lh s a bz oq & ls a kn se lse mn. p- k bo rqh & Vh \

5. vrk— lh-d' fu \ u zd lso Ks . ko lq alq l \

Now turn to Page 232 and complete the Writing Assignment.

CORRELATED LESSON FOURTEEN

31. cities s)) possibility psb)

facilities fsl)) publicity pbs)

liability lib) security sku)

maturity —tu) society ss)

necessity nec) variety vr)

pretty p) vicinity vsn)

possibilities psb))

32. brass b' kindness ki'

classes k" press p'

cross k' process ps'

doubtless dtl' promptness p—'

glass g' professor Pf'

glasses g" regardless rg/l'

gross gs' useless usl'

helpless hpl'

33. accomodate akda combined kbin

accomplished akpz commands k—— ——

accounts akts comment k—

commerce	krs	consigned	ksin̄
community	kn)	consist	ks,
compare	kpa	consistent	kss-
compel	kpl	consists	ks,,
compelled	kpl̄	consult	kslt
complaint	kpa-	constant	ks-
completely	kpel	contained	ktn̄
completing	kpl̲	contemplate	kt~pa
complied	kpī	contemplating	kt~pa̲
comply	kpi	content	kt-
complying	kpi̲	contents	kt--
confined	kfī	corn	kn
confirm	kfr~	corner	Kn
confirming	kfr~̲	correctly	krkl
consent	ks-	count	kt
considerable	Ksb	counter	K
considerably	Ksb	economy	ek~,

READING AND WRITING EXERCISE

A “h— log u bs” b —rk —ls
th vol s a kpel nu rd,\ ec
Cp ks,, v a P/ fz v ofs og\ Ks
. Cp o fl̲\ l dess nu fsl ”
sc as G kps’ fl̲ kbnls\
a fl s usl’ if l dz n kln
. kpe akls v a og\ Jp’ n
ans̲ —ral ofn dp—— pn
Jp’ n s/ & fl̲ nec Pps\
th bk l b v Ksb-hp lou rg/l’
v u lkl’\

B d Pf’—q’: —ra e lk. Lb
v sys̲ r la, bk p, of. Jp’f
us n u —k”\ ls kl̄ h— log

u bs + er s— u a kp,\
chop ul v s— k- lof\ ⌣
u ks- eʒd lk luz lh k- n
r pbs)\ r rep l b n u vsn)
⌣ n a fu ds + hl kuka ⌣
u f a apy--\ el Ks l a ki'
ful lo V. kl--\ su

Now turn to Page 234 and complete the Writing Assignment.

BASIC LESSON FIFTEEN

34. Write / to express the medial or final sound of *SHUN*, vowel-*SHUN*, *NSHUN*.

action	akj	consideration	Ksj
addition	adj	decision	dsj
additional	adjl	division	dvj
application	apkj	education	edkj
association	asZj	location	lkj
attention	alj	mention	—mj
collection	kkj	national	njl
commission	kj	notation	nlj
communication	kukj	occasion	okj
competition	kpj	position	pZj
condition	kdj	proposition	7pZj
conditions	kdjs	section	skj
connection	knkj	station	2j
connections	knkjs	suggestion	sjsj

35. Write *a* to express the sound *AU*, *AW*.

all	al	authority	A)
although	allo	fall	fal

law	*la*	talk	*lak*
saw	*sa*	walk	*wak*

Exception: ought *ol*

36. Write *a* to express initial *AN.*
Write *n* to express initial *EN, IN.*
Write *u* to express initial *UN.*

animal	*anl*	indicate	*ndka*
annual	*aul*	information	*nfy*
another	*aO*	informed	*nf̄*
enable	*nb*	instant	*ns-*
endeavor	*nDv*	instead	*nsd*
engine	*njn*	unable	*ub*
engineer	*njne*	under	*U*
enough	*nf*	understand	*Us—*
entire	*nti*	understanding	*Us═*
entirely	*ntil*	*undoubtedly	*udt̄l*
entitled	*nttl̄*	unless	*ul'*
envelope	*nvlp*		

* *The ending EDLY is expressed by joining the l to the overscore.*

READING AND WRITING EXERCISE

A. 1. ls nf lsa la ro aly zd v b
gu lo. Na lh ro\
2. il gl of l. y u ndka + fsl
llb ez l ak\
3. n adj lo. kkjv. akl lak lo
.ks ab nu bs\
4. l ol lb mj la a nj s q
nl n al pp lk a p/ n.
gvl\
5. n a skj v. la du uv.
a) lrz. fa?

B ds: u lls— nf v. akj n
n k/ lru ol f a nfl raq\
uv. a) lsk u ltak bf r
as zf\ vks ulb pd allo ev

ll —m, \ k u dsk'. la n
th kas & ls apkjlor asZf?
lgu fu nDv \ vlu

Now turn to Page 236 and complete the Writing Assignment.

CORRELATED LESSON FIFTEEN

34. accommodation
additions
anticipation
commissioner
completion
cancellation
concession
confirmation
connections
convention
conversation
correction
discussion
destination
edition
foundation
installation
motion
negotiations
objection
obligation
population
possession
preparation
production
protection
provision
recommendation
reduction
relation
reputation
sections
selection
session
vacation
valuation

35. auditor	Ad	drawing	da
author	A	drawn	dan
authorizes	Azs	haul, hall	hal
authorities	A))	laws	las
auto	als	raw	ra
automobile	alsb	talked	lak̄
ball	bal	wall	al
draw	da	altogether	allG

36. annum	a	institute	nslu
analysis	alss	insure	nzu
enabled	nb̄	intention	nl
endorse	ndrs	investigate	nvsga
endorsement	ndrs-	investigation	nvsg
endure	ndu	investment	nvs-
enjoy	njy	invited	nvō
inability	nb)	involve	nvlv
analyze	alz	involved	nvlō
indebtedness	ndld	understood	Usd
install	nsl	uniform	uf.

union	un	unfortunately	uf/nal
unit	ul	unpaid	upd
university	uvrs)		

READING AND WRITING EXERCISE

A ds: . aul kvj v. nyl asz1
v IV —frs lb hl du . tl
fal\ al y —grs r nvi\
uf/nal evb ub brec a dsj
as lolkj b l nDv lcz a
lkj kvn— f al\ udvt
s— ksj l v lb —rd f a nyl
lkj\ ezb —p lv adjl
sjsjs la l —nb us lcz a
pl\ ls r nly b—re al
nvi —sbs l. z/\ ul

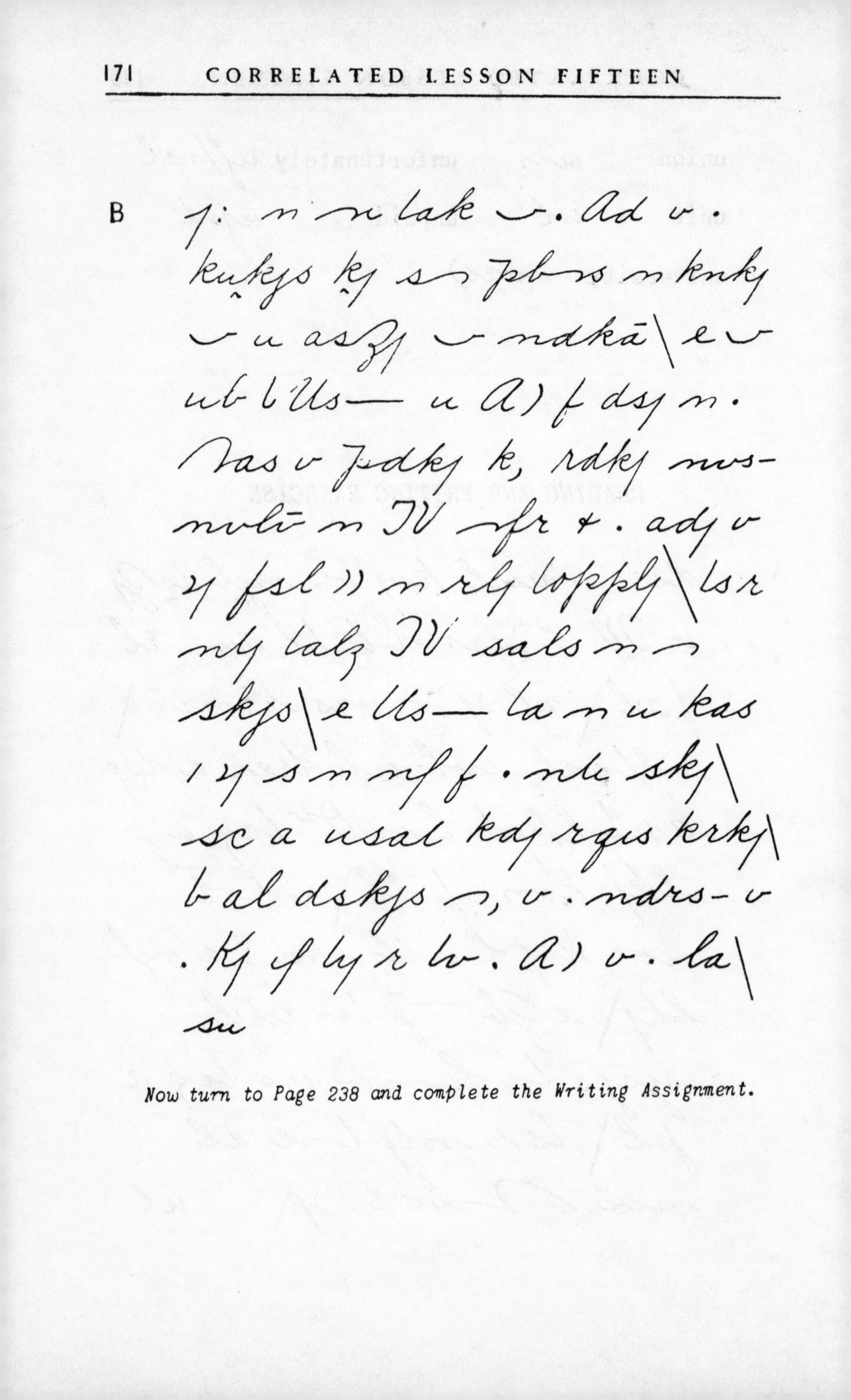

B

Now turn to Page 238 and complete the Writing Assignment.

BASIC LESSON SIXTEEN

37. Write x to express the sound of *AKS, EX, OX*.

Write X to express the sound of *EXTER, EXTIR, EXTRA, EXTRE, EXTRI, EXTRU*.

examination	xmj	explanation	xpnj
example	xmp	extension	xtj
exception	xpj	extent	xt-
exist	x,	extra	X
expert	xp/	extremely	Xml

38. Associate all the words of similar sound (families) together in your mind and thereby save the learning of separate words. Drop the final consonants *m* and *v*, and end the word with the long vowel preceding it.

claim	ka	seems	ses
name	na	home	ho
same	sa	assume	asu
*steamer	ser	presume	pzu
gave	ga	receive	rse
believe	ble	received	rsē
leave	le	receiving	rse̲
leaving	le̲		

Exception: save sav

* *When an outline begins with a comma or a capital letter, add r to express the ER ending.*

39. In words ending in the sound of *AKE*, drop the long vowel and write *k*

In words ending in the sound of the long vowel and *D*, write *d*.

In words ending in the sound of *OLD*, write *ol*.

brake	$\bar{b}k$	make	-k
break	$\bar{b}k$	take	lk

side	sd	need	nd
decide	dsd	read	rd
decided	$ds\bar{d}$	reading	$r\underline{d}$
deed	dd	grade	$\bar{g}d$
indeed	ndd	made	-d
exceedingly	$x\underline{d}l$	lading	$l\underline{d}$
lead	ld		

cold	kol	old	ol
gold	gol	sold	sol
hold	hol	told	lol

Note Bill of Lading b/l

READING AND WRITING EXERCISE

A 1. i pzu u ⌒ Zlle o. X fa ka ⌣c l ⌒k. Tp n a X⌣l Zl u\

2. lo⌣a xl- du u ble la Td n pds l n b so q as l, ⌒o?

3. pn x⌒nf v u of ifi la ek n xp gs v sc lo⌒gd\

4. sv ⌒ ⌣bs hol. pzf la adjl krss kn b v hp n. xly dvf\

5. . nd f adjl nfy s nec ldsd Lᵉ a xpf ⌒a b ⌒d\

B 1. ible ul rse a ra– v. gs
sol n. aul sal\

2. ul rse. b/l alg ⌣ a xpry
v. lu l= f pa–\

3. ⌣n erse u ⌣r el ?. gs
b f, Ja\

4. h pds̄. ol dd lo. h⌣s n
sp/ v s ‾ka\

5. f xrp i pzu uv rd.
xdl ‾ke rp/ o ⌣c r
‾ka x,,\

Now turn to Page 240 and complete the Writing Assignment.

CORRELATED LESSON SIXTEEN

37	accident	xd-	expenditure	xp— lu
	examine	x—m	expiration	xpiy
	excellent	xl-	expired	xpī
	exceptional	xpyl	export	xp/
	exceptions	xpys	extend	xt—
	excess	x'	extending	xt=
	execute	xku	external	Xnl
	exhausted	xas̄	extremity	X—)
	exhibit	xbl	oxfords	x/ll
	existing	xs̲		

38.	deem	de	game	ga
	frame	fa	steam	se

39.	lake	lk	sake	sk
	makes	-ks	takes	tks
	making	-k̲	undertakes	Utks

grades	gds	beside	bsd
laid	ld	decide	dsd
mislaid	‿sld	divide	dvd
shades	Zds	divided	dvd̄
trades	7ds	inside	nsd
feed	fd	outside	ousd
leaders	Lds	provide	pvd
leading	ld̲	providing	pvd̲
proceed	psd	sides	sds
readers	Rds	wide	‿d
reading	rd̲	load	ld
seed	sd	attitude	attd
aside	asd	food	fd
older	Ol		

ADDITIONAL WORDS

closely	ksl	nicely	nsl
face	fas	prices	pss
lease	les	trace	7as

READING AND WRITING EXERCISE

A j: wb lol la uv a hof
sal bsd. lk \ a f— as
nd f a ho ousd v
l-n \ ible lh h-s db
xl- \\ h as b X-sl l flo
a xd- + nds lrse r, +
ps \ f s sk ilō l sv
h-ss al nsl bll + n
xl- kdj \ pss v xdl
hi hv +. brss dd n
ap lb fa \ e v -lxm
. h-s lse if l s al u
—ka \ vlu

B j: bf ^ gol Ltks a x-mj v u
h-s hd lk a xprj v u brss \
d u lk s ho n ?d? hd lk

lsk a 7d lrds s xp—lu\
l asu la uk pvd a des v.
su\ af rd l h—ra dsd l
bq a xp/ — — \\ kel ll us
h— l psd af e le. nu
rd\ w —sld —n —p+
du n no. na v. rd ld
ls. lk\ ul

Now turn to Page 242 and complete the Writing Assignment.

TO THE STUDENT

By this time you have learned the importance of receiving dictation on each lesson of the course. You are now capable of writing hundreds of words automatically—without thinking. You have observed, no doubt, that you have learned the first few lessons without much difficulty; but after that, it became increasingly difficult to automatize every word you learned.

Everyone has probably experienced this problem and it is perfectly natural for this difficulty to arise. This is due to the fact that you have now reached a *plateau.* At this point it is important for you to understand that your difficulties are entirely natural, and that your inability to automatize more readily is not due to any defect in your natural make-up.

Psychologists say: You learn to swim during the winter, and to ice-skate during the summer. Although this sounds ridiculous, it has been proven to be true.

You will be able to understand this phenomenon better if you will recall the following experience. When you are hungry, you place some food into your mouth and start eating. However, the food you have just eaten does not immediately do the work for which it is intended. Without your doing anything about it, the natural process of the *assimilation* of this food within your body begins to take place. It takes many hours for the completion of this process, and it goes on without your even being conscious of it.

In the very same manner, the words you have been learning are going through a process of *mental assimilation.* When that process is completed your SPEEDWRITING shorthand will suddenly "click." While the process is going on, however, you will be experiencing many frustrations. Many a doubt will enter your mind as to your ability to master SPEEDWRITING shorthand. HAVE NO FEAR. All you need do is apply yourself with determination. Take all the dictation you can get, and it won't be long before your shorthand will "click" with you. Just keep practicing. Do the work conscientiously and you will soon be writing *automatically*—without any difficulty whatsoever.

NOTICE

If the NATIONAL REGISTRATION FORM, Page 116, is missing from Book One when you receive it from the school, write immediately to:

Speedwriting Publishing Co., Inc.
55 West 42 St., New York 36, N. Y.

Unless this form is filled in by you and registered with the national office in New York City, YOU WILL LOSE ALL LIFE-TIME TRANSFER, BRUSH-UP AND EMPLOYMENT PRIVILEGES.

KEY

to

READING AND WRITING EXERCISES

Lessons Eight to Sixteen

KEY TO CORRELATED LESSON EIGHT

A. Gentlemen:

The parcel mailed by your company came this evening. Whoever shipped it wrote South Avenue in place of South Street.

I have been greatly upset by the delay, as I had planned to give the hose for Christmas. Not only is the parcel a week late but the sizes are wrong.

I will ship the merchandise back to you and I should like to be credited for the amount of the sale.

Yours truly,

B. Dear Sir:

As you know our school won the track meet. Whenever we have the meet at this time of the year the track is lined with mud. Fearing that the men might slip, the school put off the meet till noon but the delay proved of no avail. The fellow who won slipped at the finish line and cut his head. He was cared for by the doctor associated with the school.

We have planned a show to raise money for him. We shall raise money for the school as well. Will you please buy a ticket?

Sincerely yours,

KEY TO BASIC LESSON NINE

A 1. I trust the boy will manage to sell the book for a large sum of money. I hope he will.

2. I suggest that the best style for the girl would be a suit with a fitted waist which we can manufacture at a low cost.

3. Please ask the rest of the family to join me in town on Sunday or Monday.

4. The boy has no choice. He is to study for the test on Wednesday or Thursday.

5. When will you finish the test of the oil? At this rate, the earliest we can finish is by Tuesday.

B. Gentlemen:

We will furnish the machine at cost. It will be checked between Friday and Saturday night and we shall ship it at the earliest time on Monday. We trust there will be no delay and that it will reach you in the morning on Tuesday. The department would like to assist you in getting it set up on the floor. Please state just when we should begin.

Sincerely yours,

KEY TO CORRELATED LESSON NINE

A 1. Steel reached the highest level of the year when a large tin mill raised the list price one cent a pound.

2. Again and again many metal tool companies have tried to stop the price rise hoping that the cost would stay at the level prevailing last year.

3. The State government has asked that an absolute maximum on the price of steel be set, and the plan is being studied.

B Gentlemen:

At our staff meeting last Wednesday we discussed the plan proposed by the State. We feel that it might be abused. Most of our dealing is with the finest type of men. We put the greatest trust in them. The rest, however, have not proved thoroughly honest, and would not hesitate to sell above the ceiling. This is not my only reason for refusing the plan. I suggest we meet at noon Thursday to work on a new plan, and hope you will join us in our fight.

Respectfully yours,

KEY TO BASIC LESSON TEN

A 1. In the future, I prefer a blue material for a regular summer cover for the bed. In general, it is better for every cover to be similar in color.

2. My father, mother, and brother prefer a greater voice in the policy of the newspaper. However, one particular member would rather not voice his opinion.

3. Labor would prefer a dollar an hour, but capital will offer only a higher weekly rate.

4. The writer took a longer time to give his opinion in the matter. He would turn to his father for help in the matter.

5. I hope you will wait until the weather is clearer for a sail down the river.

B Dear Sir:

We can deliver your regular newspaper to you during the summer at a low cost. No other company can do this at a lower figure. If you do not delay, our price is only 50 cents weekly. Ask to be put on our list for the delivery of "The Post". This offer is open to you for only a week. For this little sum, you are a regular member. Drop a check in the mail and the paper will reach you by Thursday.

Yours truly,

KEY TO CORRELATED LESSON TEN

A. Dear Sir:

We have realized that our club chapter is too big for the regular meeting place. We plan to build a larger club house. A chapter member, whose brother is director of a trust company, has offered to help get a mortgage. We might get a more liberal offer at a cheaper rate from the government. However, we would have to pay cash for the lot. Would you please come to the members' dinner to further work over this matter.

Yours very truly,

B. Gentlemen:

The nature of the building business is such that we cannot tell what will occur in the future. It is clearer than ever that prices will rise by summer. The longer you wait the more you will have to pay for material and labor. As you plan to build sooner or later I suggest that you go ahead without further delay. If you will refer to the folder giving building prices, you will see the sooner you build the better.

Sincerely yours,

KEY TO BASIC LESSON ELEVEN

A 1. Is it possible for you to supply me with a duplicate bill in order to pay the memorandum within the time you allow?

2. Several months ago I voiced my opinion before I supplied you with the table, a sample of which appears on Page 3.

3. As of today will you therefore cancel my order for delivery of the motor. I cannot go into the details now.

4. It is a simple matter for the manager to return the merchandise which is still available. Please inform him of the trouble in this matter.

5. Inasmuch as I filled in the form last month and did not get the merchandise, I should like to cancel my order as of today.

B 1. I return herewith the merchandise supplied to me during the past week and wish to inform you that I cannnot possibly duplicate it.

2. Because the price of steel is fixed, you have no choice in the matter. Within a month this price will not be in force.

3. The balance of the mortgage due on the building is payable within a year from now.

4. On Saturday several members were of the opinion that there was money available to pay the mortgage. This was a somewhat favorable view.

5. I suggest you inform your firm of the trouble you have had in supplying steel.

KEY TO CORRELATED LESSON ELEVEN

A. Dear May:

The pupils of Northwest High School are planning a suitable way to honor one of their former teachers. She is still capable of teaching, but because of her age she is obliged to give up teaching at Northwest. Many of the pupils would like to give a dinner in her honor. Will you please reply and tell me if you are able to assist with the details and some of the problems.

Sincerely yours,

B. Dear Bill:

I will be pleased to accompany Mrs. Gray to the dinner. Some of her former pupils have offered to bring flowers for her table. After dinner the chairman will recall the capable teaching she has done. Then there will be somebody to sing for us. In her behalf we have raised money to get her a silver travelling clock. There will be a tablet which will say simply "A teacher we will never forget."

Sincerely yours,

KEY TO BASIC LESSON TWELVE

A 1. Thank you for your check in settlement of your current bill. We will credit the payment to your firm.

2. I am certain that the president will point to sufficient support from the country for his plan.

3. In a recent shipment, your agent sent a certain supply of paint for our summer house.

4. As part of the record, they heard the report on the short supply of board for the development.

5. Courtesy should advertise an American to the world. I am certain you wish to support this judgment.

B Dear Sir:

I should like to describe the recent shipment of paint you sent to me for my winter supply. There appears to be a shortage in blue and white. Certainly you are not short of these colors in your plant. Am I right in thinking that an added shipment of the necessary colors to finish my order will be sent? Thank you for your effort in this matter.

Yours truly,

KEY TO CORRELATED LESSON TWELVE

A. Gentlemen:

Advertising men know it is necessary to base judgment on reliable data. We prepared data on every patent filed and on every plant built during the year. We give a yearly supplement of every bank statement, too.

In acknowledgment, the president of a garment firm writes, "You certainly do a good job of collecting data. It is necessary for me to get the approximate knowledge of every foreign shipment and every payment granted through government price support, and I keep informed through your monthly report."

You, too, will want the most recent report on every new development. To get a free copy, mail the attached card.

Very truly yours,

B. Dear Sir:

Shall we insert the advertisement about your building in our weekly or monthly magazine? You can guard against disappointment by setting the advertisement in large type. The description of the building is good but if the sale is urgent we suggest a more prominent heading. You might think about giving the price, too.

Sincerely yours,

KEY TO BASIC LESSON THIRTEEN

A 1. Can I depend upon you to have the shipment sent by freight at 1 P.M. Standard Time?

2. Will you kindly describe the piece of land your agents advertise in the newspaper today?

3. Please send me a description of the stocks and bonds you handle. I have in mind only late issues.

4. The custom of this firm is to handle standard merchandise at fair prices.

5. The parties to this report find that the estimate given is sound in every regard.

B 1. The mistake in the postage rates added approximately 10 cents to the cost of the copies we sent to our customers.

2. In order to sound out opinion, the magazine was sent to every part of the country.

3. Any system of cards that you handle would depend upon the kinds of records we demand.

4. The demand for stocks and bonds depends upon the rate of income they give.

5. We have found this simple system to be successful in business in most parts of the country.

KEY TO CORRELATED LESSON THIRTEEN

A. Dear Sir:

We understand that you wish to handle our line and are sending our catalogue listing standard styles and sizes of windows. Windows, square or round, may be designed to order. In such cases payment should be demanded when the order is placed so that there is no misunderstanding. Within a few months our new advertisement will appear in outstanding magazines. Before they appear on the newsstands, notices will be sent out to our agents. From the standpoint of advertising we give our dealers as much sales help as we can. On the basis of sales we can say that we have the largest selling window in the world.

Very truly yours,

B. Dear Sir:

We are happy to inform you of your appointment as trustee of Seaview School. An outline of your duties will be sent you together with notes on the proceedings of the last meeting. At the end of each calendar year you will be obliged to attend a general meeting to find out the estimated cost of maintaining buildings and grounds, and ways of raising funds. Our president sends you his kindest regards.

Sincerely yours,

KEY TO BASIC LESSON FOURTEEN

A 1. I am glad to learn that your representative will be at liberty to come and see us.

2. Always consider what is convenient for you before you complete the necessary report.

3. I should like to discuss your illness before you go to class. Please come when it is convenient for you.

4. I am confident that you wish to avoid the charge that you are too busy to discuss the committee report.

5. If you work to the best of your ability, you will find it easy to learn this system of writing.

B 1. We can now reach the city from our locality in a little less than an hour. It is very easy to get to our house.

2. When you are not too busy our representative will call on you to go over your account.

3. Throughout the year we work to the best of our capacity. However, we are happy to get a complete rest at the end of the year.

4. This is a busy organization and it is a common sight to see the men in the plant work both regular time and overtime.

5. I recommend this dress for you. You should also consider the coat to go along with it.

KEY TO CORRELATED LESSON FOURTEEN

A. "How to Organize Your Business"

by Mark Wills

This volume is a completely new study. Each chapter consists of a particular phase of office organization. Consider the chapter on filing. It describes new facilities such as large capacity filing cabinets. A file is useless if it does not contain the complete accounts of an organization. Promptness in answering mail often depends upon promptness in sorting and filing necessary papers. This book will be of considerable help to you regardless of your locality.

B. Dear Professor Glass:

May we take the liberty of suggesting our latest book, just off the press, for use in your classes. It is called "How to Organize Your Business" and we are sending you a copy. I hope you will have some comment to offer. With your consent we should like to use this comment in our publicity. Our representative will be in your vicinity within a few days, and he will communicate with you for an appointment. We will consider it a kindness if you will look over the contents.

Sincerely yours,

KEY TO BASIC LESSON FIFTEEN

A 1. It is enough to say that more attention should have been given to the matter this month.

2. I will get off at the station you indicate and from there it will be easy to walk.

3. In addition to the collection of the account, talk to the customer about new business.

4. It ought to be mentioned that a nation is great only when all people take a part in the government.

5. In what section of the law do you have the authority to raise the fare?

B Dear Sir:

You understand enough of the action now in court to write on it for a national magazine. I have the authority to ask you to talk before our association. Of course, you will be paid, although we have little money. Can you discuss the law in this case and its application to our association? Thank you for your endeavor.

Very truly yours,

KEY TO CORRELATED LESSON FIFTEEN

A. Dear Sir:

The annual convention of the National Association of Television Manufacturers will be held during the early fall. All station managers are invited. Unfortunately we have been unable to reach a decision as to location, but will endeavor to choose a location convenient for all. Undoubtedly some concession will have to be made for a national location. We shall be pleased to have additional suggestions that will enable us to choose a place. It is our intention to meet all invited members at the station.

Yours truly,

B. Gentlemen:

In my talk with the auditor of the Communications Commission some problems in connection with your association were indicated. We were unable to understand your authority for decision in the matters of production, cost reduction, investment involved in television manufacture, and the addition of station facilities in relation to population. It is our intention to analyze television sales in many sections. We understand that in your case one station is not enough for the entire section. Such an unsatisfactory condition requires correction. But all discussions must have the endorsement of the commissioner if they are to have the authority of the law.

Sincerely yours,

KEY TO BASIC LESSON SIXTEEN

A 1. I presume you wish to leave on the extra-fare car which will make the trip in an extremely short time.

2. To what extent do you believe that trade in produce will not be so great as last month?

3. Upon examination of your offer, I find that we can not accept goods of such low grade.

4. Several members hold the position that additional courses can not be of help in the extension division.

5. The need for additional information is necessary to decide whether an exception may be made.

B 1. I believe you will receive a statement of the goods sold in the annual sale.

2. You will receive the bill of lading along with an explanation of the time allowed for payment.

3. When we receive your wire, we will ship the goods by fast freight.

4. He produced the old deed to the house in support of his claim.

5. For example, I presume you have read the exceedingly clear report on which our claim exists.

KEY TO CORRELATED LESSON SIXTEEN

A. Gentlemen:

I have been told that you have a home for sale beside the lake. A friend has need for a home outside of town. I believe this house would be excellent.

He has been extremely ill following an accident and needs to receive rest and peace. For his sake I looked at several houses, all nicely built and in excellent condition. Prices were exceedingly high, however, and the terms did not appear to be fair. We want to examine the house to see if it is all you claim.

Very truly yours,

B. Gentlemen:

Before Mr. Gold undertakes an examination of your house he would like an explanation of your terms. Would you take his home in trade? He would like to make a trade to reduce his expenditure. I assume that you can provide a description of the site. After reading it he may decide to bring an expert with him. Kindly tell us how to proceed after we leave the new road. I have mislaid my map and do not know the name of the road leading to the lake.

Yours truly,

SUMMARY

of

BRIEF FORMS

Lessons One to Sixteen

SUMMARY OF BRIEF FORMS

LESSONS 1-16

about	ab	around	r–
above	bv	as	as
absolute	abs	ask	sk
acknowledge	ak	at, it	t
advertise	avz	avoid	avy
again, against	ag	because	ks
allow	l–	been	b
almost	l–so	begin	bg
already	lr	being	b–
also	lso	between	bt
always	l–	black	–b
America American	a–	both	bo
		business	bs
am	⌒	busy	bz
an	a	but buy by	b
and	&		
appear	ap		
approximate, -ly	apx	call	kl

came	k	find	fi
can	k	fine	fi
charge	cgj	for	f
child	ci	girl	g̅
children	cil	give, -n	gi
collect	kk	go, -ing	g
come, -ing	k	good	g
communicate	kuka	great	g̅
country	K	had	h
day	d	happen	hp
deal	dl	has, as	as
deliver, -ery	dl	have, -ing	v
describe	des	he, her	h
description	des	held	hl
during	du	help	hp
east	E	her, he	h
else	ls	him	⌒
easy	ez	his, is	s

hour, our	r	many	—
in, not	n	mine	mi
is, his	s	move	mv
it, at	t	necessary, -ly	nec
kind	ki	newspaper	nzp
known	no	nice	ns
labor	Lab	north	N
large	lg	not, in	n
latter	Lt	note	nt
learn	ln	object	ob
liberty	Lb	of, very	v
life	lf	on	o
like	lk	only	nl
line	li	open	op
little	ll	opinion	opn
look	lo	organize, -ation	og
magazine	mag	ought	ot
man	m-	our, hour	r

out	ou
over	V
particular, -ly	P/
piece	ps
place	pl
please	p
price	ps
prove	pv
put	p
regular, -ly	rq
represent representative	rep
result	rsl
room	rm
school	skl
several	sv
shall she ship	ʃ
small	sma
south	S
succeed	suc
success, -ful-ly	suc
table	tab
that	ta
the	
their there	7
they	ty
this	th
those	tos
thought	tt
throughout	tu
time	ti
too	to
turn	tn
until	ut

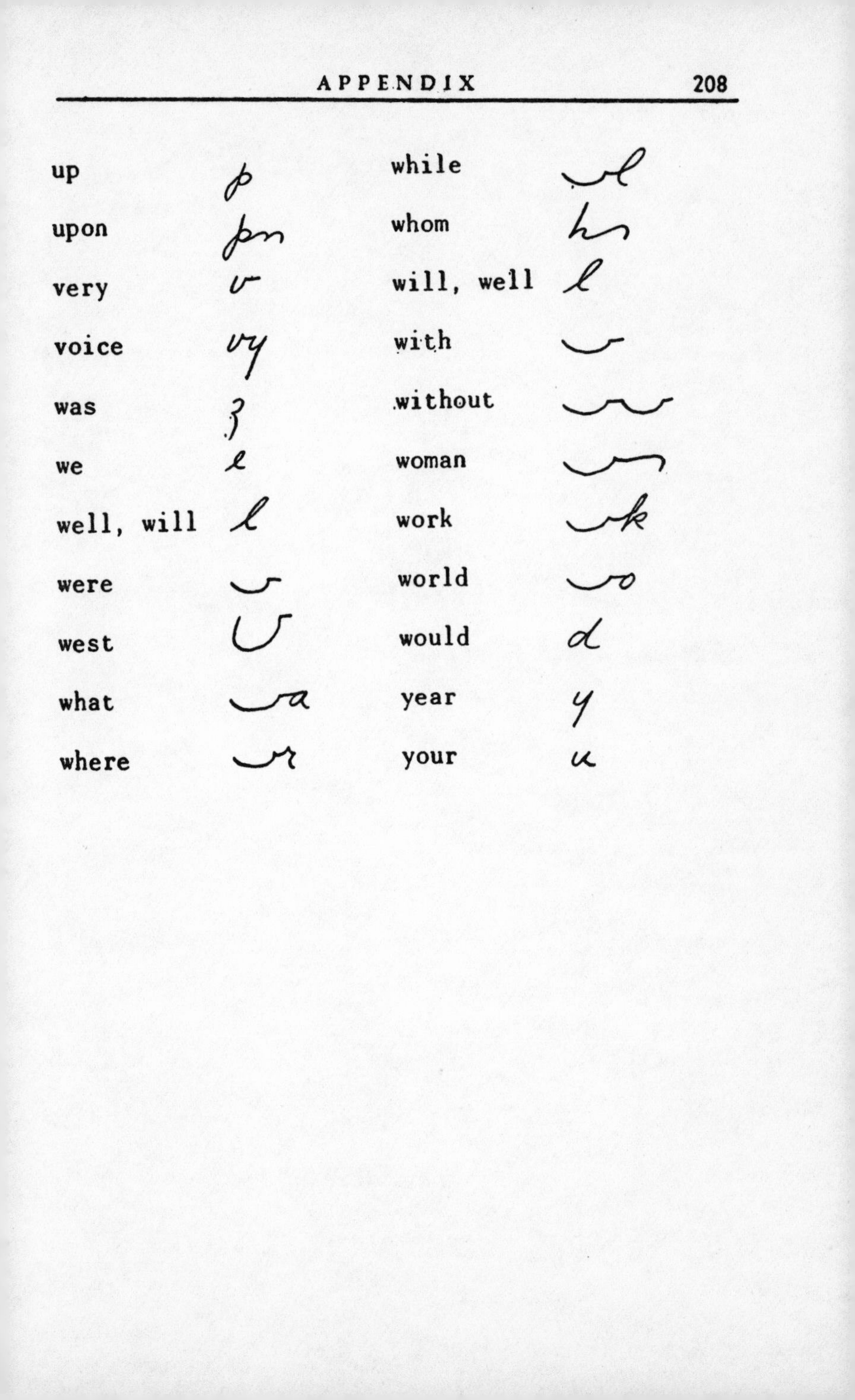

up

upon

very

voice

was

we

well, will

were

west

what

where

while

whom

will, well

with

without

woman

work

world

would

year

your

NOTICE

The following Writing Assignments are an essential part of your SPEEDWRITING Shorthand Course, and are a thorough test of your knowledge up to that point.

These Writing Assignments have been bound right into the textbooks to assure you that no matter where you study SPEEDWRITING shorthand, you are meeting the same exacting requirements which prevail throughout the country.

DO NOT USE ANY PAPER FOR THESE ASSIGNMENTS OTHER THAN THOSE BOUND INTO THE TEXTBOOK OR YOU WILL NOT RECEIVE PROPER CREDIT.

If any Writing Assignment is missing, return this book and insist upon a new, complete copy.

Name..

Date..Account No.........

WRITING ASSIGNMENT

Transcribe the following into Speedwriting for correction.

C. Dear Madam:

You write that the dozen pair of black hose you bought has not reached you. It is likely that the delay has been due to the heavy volume of Christmas mail.

My secretary will get in touch with the post office and write to you.

Yours truly,

Name..

Date..Account No.........

WRITING ASSIGNMENT

Transcribe the following into Speedwriting for correction.

C. Dear Sir:

Our choice of style is a light blue coat with a fitted waist that we manufacture at a low cost. If we can be sure of no waste, we plan to manufacture in large volume. We must figure on our capital to last at least a month.

However, we must be sure of just what we do as our company lost money on the last style we cut. Most of that merchandise did not sell well. Whenever you wish us to begin, our manager will furnish the figure on the cost to you of this style.

Yours very truly,

Name..

Date..................................Account No.........

WRITING ASSIGNMENT

Transcribe the following into Speedwriting for correction.

C. Dear John:

As you know we have leased a new house, and will be there Saturday. We are shopping for furniture and I have also bought some digging tools and a toy boat for the boy.

What we bought cost so much that we felt no joy in getting anything new.

Will you and Betty join us on Sunday to assist in getting settled.

Sincerely yours,

Name..

Date.......................................Account No.........

WRITING ASSIGNMENT

Transcribe the following into Speedwriting for correction.

C. Gentlemen:

What cover material do you have to offer for the summer months? I can order better if I see your regular catalog. Can you discover a similar material to match the color you cut for me last summer?

Mine appears to be a light blue. I plan to order for the future with little delay. If I prefer a flower material, will the cost of labor be higher?

Very truly yours,

Name..

Date....................................Account No..........

WRITING ASSIGNMENT

Transcribe the following into Speedwriting for correction.

C. Dear Sir:

The members have settled the matter of the new building. We will put up a building with an elevator, and wish to use the best materials.

As a lumber dealer you are familiar with building and it would help us to have your opinion as to whether we should build now or wait until summer, when there may be a general drop in prices.

Sincerely yours,

Name..

Date...Account No..........

WRITING ASSIGNMENT

Transcribe the following into Speedwriting for correction.

C. Gentlemen:

Will you cancel my order for the table as of today inasmuch as the cost of this particular object is higher than I paid a year ago. I know that your company has had labor trouble which has forced a higher price.

As of today, therefore, it will cost me $10 more. Is it possible that the cost will be lower within a year? Can you possibly offer a discount on the original table now? If you can give me a favorable reply, wire me today.

Sincerely yours,

Name..

Date..Account No..........

WRITING ASSIGNMENT

Transcribe the following into Speedwriting for correction.

C. Gentlemen:

Figures show that one of the chief problems of shipping is the delay in removal of merchandise from ships to the warehouse. Delivery is sometimes overdue. Supplies are sometimes held up for weeks.

Wholesale dealers state that they will not be liable for overcharge because of delay. They say that if shippers cannot be more reliable they will cancel orders. Would it be reasonable to cable salesmen informing them when foreign supplies are available?

Yours truly,

Name...

Date...Account No...........

WRITING ASSIGNMENT

Transcribe the following into Speedwriting for correction.

C. Dear Madam:

I happen to know that the members of the board will support the president of the bank in regard to the method for payment of the mortgage.

In the judgment of the president, part payment in cash is necessary before a settlement can be reached. It will then be sufficient to pay the balance due in five years by paying a small amount each month. Let me know what you think.

Yours very truly,

Name..........,..

Date.......................................Account No..........

(There is no Writing Assignment for Correlated Lesson 12)

WRITING ASSIGNMENT

Transcribe the following into Speedwriting for correction.

C. Gentlemen:

The paper you shipped was delivered to me today, but I fear that I shall not be able to handle it. I handle a standard weight paper that is not too dear. The paper you sent is too cheap for my customers.

Kindly supply me with samples of a good bond paper in every color. Let me know where I stand as regards price. My stock is running low and I depend upon you for most of the paper I handle.

Sincerely yours,

Name...

Date..................................Account No.........

WRITING ASSIGNMENT

Transcribe the following into Speedwriting for correction.

C. Gentlemen:

Recent tests show that our window is more air tight than the requirements of the Bureau of Weights and Standards demand. Our new booklet, recording the results of these findings, is intended for agents who handle our line.

We can send you copies depending on your wants. If it suits you, bound samples are available for your customers. We will pay the postage. Our calendar is also available for your plants and offices.

Sincerely yours,

Name...

Date...Account No.........

WRITING ASSIGNMENT

Transcribe the following into Speedwriting for correction.

C. Gentlemen:

We were informed that the price of steel will rise during the last six months of this year. This will force a higher price for almost every object throughout our line. To meet the higher costs, our charges will go up as much as two cents a foot.

In our judgment, your firm should buy without delay the material you consider necessary for the rest of the year. These common items can be supplied now with little or no added cost to you. If you wish, you can give our agent a list of these items for your account.

Yours truly,

Name..

Date..Account No..........

WRITING ASSIGNMENT

Transcribe the following into Speedwriting for correction.

C. Dear friend:

For shoe comfort we recommend the White Cross Shoe. Foot doctors state that these shoes are designed to give the greatest comfort.

Though this brand is generally considered beyond the reach of the average customer, it is now available for considerably less than regular low-priced shoes. Such a price represents a considerable loss to us. Yet regardless of the loss we are compelled to clear our counters.

Sincerely yours,

Name..

Date....................................Account No.........

WRITING ASSIGNMENT

Transcribe the following into Speedwriting for correction.

C. Gentlemen:

I should like to mention the matter of your account which is now long past due. In your communication of a month ago, you thought you could have this account settled by this time.

In this envelope we are sending another statement to indicate the sum due. We shall be glad if you will kindly forward a check to cover the entire amount.

Yours very truly,

Name..

Date..Account No.........

WRITING ASSIGNMENT

Transcribe the following into Speedwriting for correction.

C. Dear Sir:

In a conversation with local authorities I learned that your information is in error. Application for another station is now under consideration by the Federal Communications Commission. They will soon authorize the new installation.

In anticipation of their action negotiations are now under way. Completion of another station will insure competition. The public is entitled to enjoy it and it is our obligation to present it. Instead of filling the entire day with advertising, we ought to allow air time for education.

Yours truly,

Name..

Date....................................Account No..........

WRITING ASSIGNMENT

Transcribe the following into Speedwriting for correction.

C. Dear Sir:

We can make an exception in your case and take a small payment on account. We do not wish to believe that you want to avoid payment of this invoice for too long a time.

Such a position would give your firm a bad credit rating and we would be forced to take orders only for cash. I assume we will receive a check for the balance in a very short time. Thank you for the payment on the old bill.

Sincerely yours,

Name..

Date...Account No.........

WRITING ASSIGNMENT

Transcribe the following into Speedwriting for correction.

C. Dear Sir:

I was exceedingly happy to receive your communication referring to our lakeside homes. Several have been sold. We plan to break ground for new brick units on land extending to the lake. If I may presume to make a suggestion, I believe that these seem better suited to your friend than the older frame houses.

All will be the same price. One wide lot with several shade trees extends for eighty feet. It may be sold in one piece or divided. Your friend may take possession when the deed is executed.

Yours very truly,